INFINITY HOUSE

AN ENDLESS VIEW

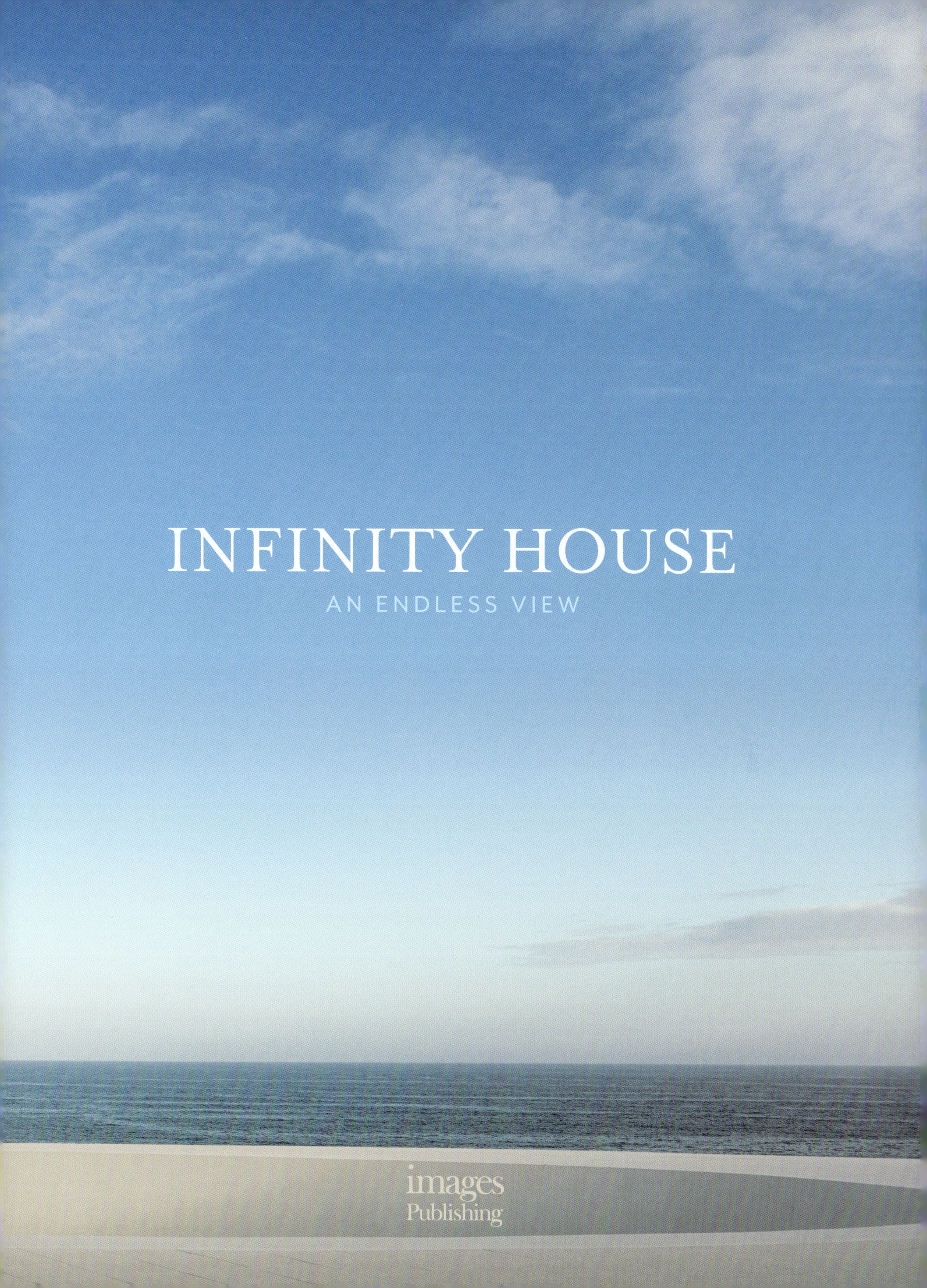

INFINITY HOUSE

AN ENDLESS VIEW

images
Publishing

CONTENTS

9 INTRODUCTION CATHI HOUSE

12 SWEEPING BAY VIEWS OAKLAND, CA, UNITED STATES

20 RELAXED VISTAS AUSTIN, TX, UNITED STATES

28 REVISITING TRADITION URBINO, ITALY

36 ATLANTIC VISION CAPE TOWN, SOUTH AFRICA

44 RIVER CANYON LOS ANGELES, CA, UNITED STATES

52 PANORAMIC PERFECTION CABO SAN LUCAS, MEXICO

60 ALIEN LANDSCAPE ANCÓN, PERU

68 SOARING ABOVE LOS ANGELES, CA, UNITED STATES

76 ORGANIC SCULPTURE LAGOS, PORTUGAL

84 FRAMING THE VIEW MINORCA, SPAIN

92 ON EVERY LEVEL NEWCASTLE, NSW, AUSTRALIA

100 BRIDGE BETWEEN ANTIPAROS, GREECE

108 ON SOLID ROCK FORMENTERA, SPAIN

116 THE INFINITE SEA CÁDIZ, SPAIN

124 CARIBBEAN IDYLL HARBOUR ISLAND, THE BAHAMAS

132 SIMPLE DECEPTION MNÍŠEK, CZECH REPUBLIC

140 LION'S PRIDE CAPE TOWN, SOUTH AFRICA

148 WINDSWEPT JERSEY, UNITED KINGDOM

156 FLOATING ABOVE LOS ANGELES, CA, UNITED STATES

166 EASY LIVING CAPE TOWN, SOUTH AFRICA

174 COASTAL ESCARPMENT GERRINGONG, NSW, AUSTRALIA

182 MOUNTAINSIDE MARVEL MASSIF DU CHARLEVOIX, QC, CANADA

190 NATURAL INTEGRATION JACKSON HOLE, WY, UNITED STATES

198 VINEYARD BEAUTY HEALDSBURG, CA, UNITED STATES

206 ARRANGING THE VIEW VANCOUVER, BC, CANADA

214 SEASIDE SERENITY NHA TRANG, VIETNAM

222 CONNECTING THE VIEWS VANCOUVER, BC, CANADA

230 LOFTY GLAMOR LOS ANGELES, CA, UNITED STATES

238 PERENNIAL BLISS ISTEBNA, POLAND

246 SERIES OF VIEWS PAROS, GREECE

254 EAGLE'S VIEWPOINT MALLORCA, SPAIN

262 PROJECT CREDITS

INTRODUCTION

CATHI HOUSE

The world we live in is a wondrous place filled with so many pleasures for the soul. The changing shades of sky and water on an isolated shore, the whisper of wind in grasses, the rustle of leaves, the calls of water birds as they soar above, the luminous glow of the sky at sunrise, the quiet of a still afternoon. Nourishing our senses by focusing on these pleasures can renew our appreciation for life, calm our anxieties, and help us focus on the joy, wonder, and surprise to be found in every day. The stunning homes in this beautiful collection give us glimpses into what a world filled with these pleasures might look like. The designs are as different as the lands they occupy. From steep city hillsides and isolated lakes to jungle-covered islands and stark rocky cliffs, each home responds to its setting with respect, poetry, warmth, and comfort, offering their occupants the opportunity to truly focus on the beauty of our world.

The architectural styles vary from the simple shapes of a local vernacular barn to highly sculpted form-as-art; the materials used range from crisp stucco to natural wood, to steel, and rustic stone. Some of these homes sit in landscapes that are vast and lonely, others in densely developed neighborhoods. H_orizon incorporates the crisp white vernacular of the Greek Islands. It sits in a rugged landscape that embraces the home and reflects in a serene pool, bold yet barely touching the land into which it so carefully weaves itself. Cut into the earth to reveal the texture of its land, House on Formentera Island frames spectacular views of the sea. Logie Point's two homes stand boldly apart, yet are completely integrated into the landscape with transparent rooms of stone, wood, and glass looking to the gardens and the sea. The property is fully off-grid with advanced technology, complemented by grassy roofs and a reed-filled pond. A palette of warm materials in A House with a View frames the vista to the city below. An olive tree set in a fountain as the foreground to Devlin draws the vista through transparent spaces of floor-to-ceiling glass to the distant view of twinkling lights. OVD525 is accessed through a series of layered, textured walls that conceal, then reveal the beautifully crafted wood and steel spaces that focus on an endless sea. Orum Residence uses a specimen tree in a sober swath of stone paving to create a calm central focal point that counters the vast and complex view over the city.

Several of these homes are modest and respectful of local vernacular. The Range's minimalist form of a steel-clad farm building set on a stone plinth in softly rolling hills with views to the sea offers a gentle embrace to the occupants, where each space has its own view focused to different aspects of the site. The scale and simplicity of House on a Dune offers no hint of the powerful broad expanses of view to the jungle and the sea from within, where open shaded spaces are peaceful, protective, and completely embraced by nature. In Casa C3 simple, powerful forms touch the boulders of its rugged site with delicate grace.

Casa Ambar's curving shape and undulating trellis is reminiscent of a bird perched to take flight over the city below. Elliptic House is a swirl of carefully calculated geometries that lend each space a unique composition through which to experience its manicured lawns and panorama of the sea, the roof capturing an elliptical perspective of the constantly changing sky. Complex, multilayered homes like Beyond use foldaway walls to extend vistas to the garden and sea, while Blue Jay Way employs a peaceful reflecting pool around a shaded lawn for a serene vista over an expanse of city lights.

Two important considerations in the design of a home are how well it responds to the nature and needs of the inhabitants, and how well it is adapted to its setting. As to how a residence responds to the owners—their hopes, dreams, habits, idiosyncrasies—that is a process for each architect to discover and develop. But how well a home responds to the essence of its particular site—forces such as sun, wind, rain, topography, vegetation, views, and neighboring homes—these elements are not variable. In fact, they are so set that predictability makes it simple to incorporate appropriate responses into the design. It is this strong connection to nature that each of these homes have in common and what sets them apart from the mass-produced suburban houses that lack site-specific thought and litter our world with blandness and unsustainability. Meticulous site analysis is one of the most important guiding principles an architect can employ to design a home that is well-suited to its setting. The decisions developed through this thoughtful study can provide ample assistance with neighborhood review boards focused on keeping things the same, clarifying how design choices in orientation, fenestration and materials can allow for the evolution of homes and communities toward a more sustainable future.

While each home presented in this volume is unique, they share one important quality. In this tech-driven era of fast-paced, long working hours, these homes give us a glimpse into a possible future where the spaces we inhabit can reconnect us to nature and the calm introspection that this invites—where days can be judged by the shade and texture of the water or the patterns of clouds in a luminous sky, where the sounds of birds and wind become part of the music of our lives and natural light washing across our walls is more beautiful than the art on those walls. Whether simple in form or boldly sculpted, each of these homes offers the people that live within the opportunity to truly focus on the beauty of their environment. More importantly, they show us a way back to a relationship with nature and the peacefulness, surprise, and joy of simply being more linked to the world around us.

Cathi House, Architect
House + House Architects

For over thirty-five years, co-founders of House + House Architects, Cathi and Steven House, have crafted intimate, personal architecture reflecting their passion for site-specific, well-choreographed buildings throughout California, Mexico, and the Caribbean. In 1989 *Architecture* magazine featured House + House in its "Discovery" issue on emerging talent. Since then they have received over fifty design awards and their work has been featured in numerous publications, including two monographs, *House + House Architects: Choreographing Space* and *Houses in the Sun: light movement embrace*. Cathi and Steven's extensive studies of vernacular architecture have been published in two very personal memoirs, *Mediterranean Villages: an architectural journey* and *Villages of West Africa: an intimate journey across time*. They have established CASA (The Center for Architecture, Sustainability + Art), a study abroad program based in Mexico.

SWEEPING BAY VIEWS

OAKLAND, CA, UNITED STATES

Referring to this residence as "A House with a View" may well be seen as a bit of an understatement. Perched high on a hillside, the house enjoys a sweeping and spectacular vista over the city of Oakland, and the San Francisco East Bay.

While technically the result of a renovation to reconfigure and open up the entire back elevation, the results arguably speak for themselves. The effect is expansive, opening the house up to the light and unveiling the dramatic views of the bay.

For the interior design, the palette consists of contrasting dark wood flooring and white walls, and cabinetry throughout, creating a monochromatic and striking feel within the space. Indoor-outdoor living flows onto the large exterior decking, matching the internal stained black oak wood flooring to the blackened cedar wood outdoor deck, which provides a place to take in the views. A louvered screen by the entrance separates the entry area from the living space, while providing a glimpse of the dramatic bay scenery beyond.

The entrance to the house is reached via a pathway that wraps around a centenarian redwood tree, purposely retained during the building work. Upon entering, the doorway frames the view of a light, bright living space and a panorama of the bay. A large, ample dining and living space stretches across the entire back of the house, taking advantage of the incredible views, both day and night.

"The doorway frames the view of a light, bright living space and a panorama of the bay."

A HOUSE WITH A VIEW *by* AXELROD ARCHITECTS

ROTHK

VANITY FAIR 100 YEARS
ANNIE LEIBOVITZ A Photographer's Life 1990–2005
PHOTOGRAPHS BY STEFAN MAY
CLASSIC CARS
PARIS

RELAXED VISTAS

AUSTIN, TX, UNITED STATES

Stretching across a bluff with dazzling views of the Colorado River, this contemporary yet relaxed home boasts a stunning vista from every room.

The design is really about the panoramic water views unfolding just beyond the back of the house while at the same time creating a space that is modern yet comfortable, and seamlessly blends the indoors and outdoors. This connection is evident particularly in the long pocketing floor-to-ceiling retractable glass door that disappears into the walls to fully open up the living room and kitchen directly to the outdoors.

Despite its generous size, the home feels intimate and personal. Carefully curated furnishings complement the contemporary architecture while remaining casual and durable. Concrete floors add to the easy-going personality of the home, while redwood finishes outside and white oak inside reflect the riverside setting. The landscaping echoes the home's relaxed nature with indigenous plants, and the Texas-sourced Antique Lueders Limestone finishing the exterior walls roots the home firmly in its setting.

All in all the elements and design combine to create a non-fussy feel that meshes with the personalities of the owners, resulting in an understated elegance that perfectly reflects the lifestyles of its owners, who state, "This house is for having fun and making memories in."

NELO
ALBUM RELEASE

"The design is really about the panoramic water views."

ABOVE THE LAKE *by* DICK CLARK + ASSOCIATES

REVISITING TRADITION

URBINO, ITALY

Boasting a superb setting on the top of one of the highest hills in Urbino, this house marks the rebirth of an ancient rural hamlet in an area highly esteemed for its landscape and environment. And just one look across to the distant mountains confirms why. The views are picture-postcard perfect.

The new building stands on ancient remains, dating back to medieval times. The beautiful stone volume rests on a red concrete platform, evoking the color of terra cotta tiles so prevalent in Italy's architectural history. The considered design, with its measured proportions and free of external distractions such as gutters or drainpipes, speaks to the historical typologies of the region, and forms a central role in restoring a direct and empathic dialogue between the new construction and historical stratification. The resultant picture is one that faithfully reinterprets the typical formal architectural themes of this particular Italian region. Here is a structure that fits seamlessly into the landscape, resting easily on the centuries of building tradition yet offering a convincing vindication of its place in the modern world. Even the garage is located in the basement, to avoid the sight of cars.

In contrast to its traditional stone exterior, the interior consists of generous expanses of concrete, offering a cool respite from the sun's heat in summer. Large glazed windows offer framed views of the spectacular rolling hills in the distance. The modern bespoke furniture was created by GGA architects, and is made of natural walnut wood.

But it is the outside that calls to you. The benches placed enticingly on the red concrete platform encourage one to sit and take in the view.

"Large glazed windows offer framed views of the spectacular rolling hills in the distance."

AP HOUSE URBINO *by* GGA GARDINI GIBERTINI ARCHITETTI

ATLANTIC VISION

CAPE TOWN, SOUTH AFRICA

This stunning residence shows the impressive result when the full comfort of a modern home is potently married to an elemental architecture drawn from its dramatic setting.

Perched on the shoulders of Lion's Head, Beyond springs from a steep hillside that drops off to the famous sequence of Clifton's white beaches. The interior contains a masterful interplay of light, space, and raw materiality, from the cavernous entrance hall to the upper levels that are bathed in generous daylight.

The glazed lines between inside and out peel back to blur the boundaries in a continuous transparent space that links a generous back garden to a pool that stretches out toward the sea in front. And it is here that the view out over the ocean comes into its own, particularly at dusk.

The fortunate residents can relax in the dining room and lounge on the fourth floor, which transforms into an extension of the open terrace via glass sliding doors, allowing unfettered views to the distance. The angular modern bar with bar lounge is suspended over the pool, with the beautiful panorama framed by the ocean-facing window. With its sleek, modern lines, the house finds a reflection both literally and metaphorically in the crisp lines of the infinity pool, from where one can gaze out over the mercurial waters of the Atlantic.

"Nearly every room showcases panoramic views of the Atlantic Ocean."

BEYOND *by* SAOTA

RIVER CANYON

LOS ANGELES, CA, UNITED STATES

This stunning residence is set in a neighborhood of Los Angeles often associated with musicians and movie stars. But rather than rubbing shoulders with the Hollywood elite, the inhabitants enjoy a spacious yet private luxury residence and a view down to the city's Sunset Strip.

The overall design can be described as crisp and comfortable, with clearly defined edges and surfaces. The house is shielded from the street by dense vegetation, assuring privacy. Full-height glazing allows the inhabitants to relish the spectacular view and also emphasizes the indoor-outdoor design that takes full advantage of the benign climate.

Rather unusually, the home is bisected by a pool and water feature, in response to the client's request. This constraint was turned into a design feature, as the architect imagined the home as a "canyon, deep and narrow with a river running through it." Beginning with a water wall near the entry, the pool ends with an infinity drop-off. An outdoor terrace and lounging area provides the perfect place for relaxing while drinking in the cityscape vista.

"Full-height glazing allows the inhabitants to relish the spectacular view."

BLUE JAY WAY *by* MCCLEAN DESIGN

PANORAMIC PERFECTION

CABO SAN LUCAS, MEXICO

This curved house holds an enviable position, sitting atop a rugged mountain at the tip of the Baja Peninsula, overlooking the nearby city and the Pacific Ocean. Stepped to fit the sloping site, the house sits deep into the earth for natural cooling while providing 280 degrees of arresting views of ocean, town, and desert.

Entry is via an arched shade that leads to open stairs that curve down a story to the main living spaces. The stairs end at an outdoor vestibule and grotto with surprising views across the great room to a continuous wall of folding glass and a full-width shaded terrace. This main space, with kitchen, dining, and lounge, arcs to follow the expansive view. The terrace is split with more outdoor stairs, these leading to the lower bedroom terrace, and infinity pool.

This sustainable house, designed by Mark Simon, Todd Andrews, and Justin Hedde of Centerbrook, was built using indigenous masonry construction of concrete and block, all covered in white stucco. This reflects the intense heat on the outside while maintaining cooler temperatures within, through the thermal storage of the heavy mass and earth behind.

With the glass doors open, the great room and terrace become one indoor-outdoor space with panoramic views to the east, south, and west. The floating canopy above the terrace uses traditional woven bamboo "latilla," providing dappled shading. The terrace itself is wide, with glass rails, to frame a view of nothing but ocean, without a hint of the community downhill.

The upper terrace overhangs to provide shade while the long narrow infinity pool arcs across the edge of the lower terrace, again blocking views of all but the Pacific Ocean and (if you're in luck) its spouting whales.

"This stunning design provides 280 degrees of arresting views of ocean, town, and desert."

CASA AMBAR *by* CENTERBROOK

CAMINO
EL CIELO

ALIEN LANDSCAPE

ANCÓN, PERU

An exercise in design restraint, Casa C3 is situated in Marina Lancheros in Ancón, a popular beach resort in the northern Lima province. Its surrounding landscape is stark, almost Martian-like, and the architects sought to create a house that was an expression of the rocky land and the cliff-edge location.

The Peruvian desert stands at the confluence of the Andes mountain range and the Pacific Ocean, which creates a unique climate: highly humid, although without any rain, with constant temperatures all year long.

The house soaks up and reflects the native elements of its environment—the reddish soil, the gray rock, and the sparse vegetation. Rather than being simply an object in the landscape, the structure was designed to appear as part of the natural environment.

You might think that the views would form the main focus during the planning process, but the architects decided that framing the fabulous views was not the main priority. Instead, they focused on creating a microcosm that would allow an understanding of its unique features through the revelation of its hidden qualities.

Local and non-specialized craftsmanship was used in the construction, including stone masonry and the use of local pozzolanic cement, which bestows a reddish color, allowing the house to blend in with the surrounding cliffs.

Although capturing the wide vistas was not the main priority during the design, spaces were included where the inhabitants can enjoy the views, comfortably ensconced in their stark, basic, yet beautiful house, and surrounded by a seemingly alien landscape.

"The house soaks up and reflects the native elements of its environment—the reddish soil, the gray rock, and the sparse vegetation."

CASA C3 *by* BARCLAY & CROUSSE ARCHITECTURE

SOARING ABOVE

LOS ANGELES, CA, UNITED STATES

A beautiful view deserves an equally beautiful design, and here again McClean Design delivers the goods with a modern and streamlined luxurious home. With sweeping views to downtown Los Angeles, this house successfully capitalizes on the available outlook.

The entry sequence to the house includes a water feature with an olive tree, intended to create a transition between the street and the entrance. Residents and visitors enter through a double-story space that immediately opens to a view of the city below. The main spaces here offer access to the garden and the terrace, while the pool cantilevers over the sloped site and curves to match the contours of the property. According to the architects, "The continuous opening is the largest we have ever attempted and creates a situation where the entire lower level opens to the rear yard, connecting the house to the exterior environment."

The view over the infinity pool almost gives an impression of being in flight above the city, directly below. Meanwhile, the large interior living spaces allow ample room to enjoy life, all set against the dramatic backdrop of the urban landscape beyond.

"Entry is via a double-story space that immediately opens to a view of the city below."

DEVLIN *by* MCCLEAN DESIGN

TOM
FORD

ORGANIC SCULPTURE

LAGOS, PORTUGAL

With its elliptical base, this house is deliberately sculptural and organic. It is seemingly shaped by the wind and the sea, which wants to embrace the wide floating oval. This unique design also provides a spectacular site for gazing across the brilliant blue ocean.

The entrance hall is central and open, with direct access to all living areas. From there, the eye is drawn to the water surface of the pools, which merges visually with the vastness of the sea, directly in front. The living area continues to an outside patio, framed by the emptiness of the ellipse that gives the house its shape. This intriguing empty void offers shade on the patio as shadows gradually move across during the course of the day. The overall interior color scheme is a calming and refreshing white.

The outdoor terraces, paved or landscaped, are at various levels and seem to disappear into the garden, offering a defined line over the changing waters of the ocean. And so the interior flows out to the patios and terraces and into the Mediterranean landscape. It is in this ambience that the house should be experienced, without being aware of where the house begins and ends. The fluidity and lightness of its organic design reflects natural shapes, thus defining the house architecturally in its natural setting, while the inhabitants enjoy distinctive views that stretch out across the watery horizon, framed by different angles of the organic design.

"With its elliptical base, the house is deliberately sculptural and organic."

ELLIPTIC HOUSE *by* MÁRIO MARTINS ATELIER

FRAMING THE VIEW

MINORCA, SPAIN

In order to truly take advantage of this steep plot, which has a magnificent view over the sea, the architects pushed the house back to the highest point so as to avoid the views being blocked by a neighboring home. The results clearly justify this decision, with an unhampered view over the landscape to the brilliantly blue waters.

To further guarantee the view, the sleeping areas were located on the ground floor while the main living spaces were placed on the first floor; with the exception of the master bedroom, that is, which was positioned on the top floor, transforming the holiday home into a sort of single loft with an extension for the rest of the family below.

The strong contrast between the openness of the sea-view façade and the opacity of the side and back façades creates a strong framing effect. To further enhance this gesture the roof is inclined opening up toward the view and the whole front façade is glazed from floor to ceiling with large sliding windows. As well, large sliding windows in the kitchen and living room open up to a terrace where the inhabitants can gather together. The façade is covered with concrete, chosen for its zero-maintenance qualities and ability to cope with Minorca's aggressive climate of humidity and high salt levels. The off-white façade blends in with the terra cotta colored soil surrounding the home.

One suspects it is the terrace, with its stunning view across the lower landscape, where the residents spend their time, relishing the contrast between the white façade and the green and blue beyond.

"The architects pushed the house back to the highest point in order to avoid the views being blocked."

FRAME HOUSE *by* NOMO STUDIO

ON EVERY LEVEL

NEWCASTLE, NSW, AUSTRALIA

Build a house in front of an ocean and everything becomes about the view. Located close to the ocean cliffs in Merewether, Newcastle, Greenacres responds to both site and location. Set on a steep block, the varying heights created the opportunity for multiple platforms to view the expansive outlook over the ocean, the Merewether Ocean Baths, and the city of Newcastle.

Stepping down a steep gradient at three levels the house works with the landscape as it terraces down the hill toward the street. The garage is buried at the base of the property, with the entry path and garden weaving beside, up, and over the top, through the green roof. The design of the driveway is landscaped to reduce the impact of a large expanse of hard surface in front of the house. A simple, white rectangular form, propped on three giant steel "paperclips," houses the kitchen/living and dining area, with two bedrooms and a bathroom beneath.

At Greenacres the deliberate transparency ensures the house never gets in the way of its own view. While sitting in the back garden, working in the study, or showering in the very last room on the block, the great expanse of city and ocean is unimpeded.

"Build a house in front of an ocean and everything becomes about the view."

GREENACRES *by* AUSTIN MAYNARD ARCHITECTS

BRIDGE BETWEEN

ANTIPAROS, GREECE

Located on a beautiful Cycladic island, this house anchors on the landscape, creating a bridge between the sea and the land, with panoramic views over the Aegean Sea.

The name H_orizon derives not only from the H-shaped configuration but also from the design aim for the house to remain in continuous connection to the open horizon beyond. The open void between the two main volumes creates a frame that captures the perpetual energy and alternating images of the sea. This element remains as a focal point of the house that concentrates on daily family activity and movements of the natural scenery. At the same time it is the point from which the viewpoints begin and extend.

The house emerges from the landscape and the landscape evolves linearly as an extension of the house. Views are maximized throughout the interior spaces, such as the picturesque framed view from the sunken lounge, deliberately in a recessed level to allow for unobscured access. White walls typical of traditional Greek lime-wash buildings serve to enhance the blue of the sea. The streamlined interior is discretely furnished, and the wooden doors provide a warm contrast to the white walls and the internal polished concrete floors. The infinity pool situated in front of the living area follows the linear direction toward the horizon, and provides a bridge between the two blue surfaces of water. Seating areas adjacent to the pool provide the perfect spot to soak up the surrounding Greek landscape and lose yourself gazing off into the distance.

"The open void creates a frame that captures the perpetual energy and alternating images of the sea."

H_ORIZON *by* VOIS ARCHITECTS

ON SOLID ROCK

FORMENTERA, SPAIN

With views to the beautiful turquoise waters of the ocean, this house, on the south coast of the island and handily located next to the beach of Migjorn, is set in a landscape that unleashes a desire to gaze toward the distant horizon.

The design of the home focuses on the duality of its combined elements; the heavy and the light, the handcrafted and the technological. The house is placed on a rock, which looks as if it has been carved, and comprises three light modules, clad with wood, and a space carved out below. The construction of the residence was careful to remain sensitive to the surrounding environment. Perhaps as a reward for their caution, the architects were surprised and delighted to discover a natural cave in the main courtyard, which was enthusiastically integrated into the overall design during construction.

The interior is a soothing mix of birch wood paneling and crisp white. The design is minimalist, helping to create a relaxing and soothing place to unwind and retreat from the heat of the day. A large covered overhang provides shelter from the sun and wind, and a comfortable spot to contemplate the view over the light green bushes to the blue waters.

"The design of the home focuses on the duality of its combined elements."

HOUSE ON FORMENTERA ISLAND *by* MARIÀ CASTELLÓ MARTÍNEZ

THE INFINITE SEA

CÁDIZ, SPAIN

Situated on the edge of the coast, facing the infinite waters of the Atlantic, sits this radical house, designed to appear as a stone platform, or jetty.

This horizontal plane appears bare and denuded by choice to preserve the straight lines, and faces the distant horizon. In order to achieve this dream, much engineering work was required. The large box that forms the front of the house hides a further two floors, excavated into the solid rock, which hosts the living space. On the denuded stone platform, three walls provide protection from the strong prevailing winds that rush in off the ocean waters.

Described as a podium house, "all podium, only podium," it provides a sense of certainty against the wild landscape of its surroundings, with its perfectly straight and perfectly horizontal lines.

A house of the infinite, on an infinite plane facing the infinite sea. What a wonderful place to sip a local sherry while gazing out into the great beyond.

"A house of the infinite, on an infinite plane facing the infinite sea."

HOUSE OF THE INFINITE *by* ALBERTO CAMPO BAEZA

CARIBBEAN IDYLL

HARBOUR ISLAND, THE BAHAMAS

A house on a dune on a Caribbean island with enviable vistas over the turquoise waters of the tropical ocean is the stuff of dreams. And with this understated simple residence, it becomes a happy reality.

Situated on the relaxed yet luxurious Harbour Island, the architecture for this private residence is conceived as simultaneously powerful, yet comfortable; primitive, yet innovative; casual, yet elegant; raw, yet refined. The result is a sensual and sensitive experience, reduced to its essence through the use of elemental forms and sincere materiality and detailing. The most dramatic view of the ocean is obtained toward the crest of the dunes, the location of this modest home.

The central space of the house is essentially an open breezeway, allowing visual and pedestrian connectivity across the site. Within this pavilion space there is the living and dining area that open onto verandas well protected from the elements by the deep overhangs of the gabled roof. The rest of the living spaces are simply arranged around the central space. To the left are two guest suites with private bathrooms; while to the right are the kitchen area and the master suite.

This private residence establishes a delicate, meditative, and mediating space that ushers in a transition from lush tropic landscape to wide languorous ocean, and moves from the welcome shadows of the interior out to the Caribbean sun and the blue water expanse.

"This private residence establishes a space that ushers in a transition from lush tropic landscape to wide languorous ocean."

HOUSE ON A DUNE *by* OPPENHEIM ARCHITECTURE

SIMPLE DECEPTION

MNÍŠEK, CZECH REPUBLIC

The property, located on a mountain ridge in the tiny hamlet of Mníšek in the Ore Mountains, just near the German border, offers a one-of-a-kind panoramic view.

The deceptively simple house is of a traditional type, consisting of two floors with a gabled roof. Thanks to the property's excellent orientation, the living spaces open up to the surrounding vistas while also letting in sunlight. The local access road follows the property's northern border, with unique stunning views to the south.

The expansive main living room is lined with large floor-to-ceiling windows. The short summer season inspired the addition of a covered terrace in the central part of the southwestern façade that can be accessed from the living and dining rooms. Thanks to a large sliding window, the space can be permanently opened during the warm season. It has become the heart of the house. A single-flight staircase next to the winter garden leads to the upper floor.

While the interior is characterized by the use of wood and light colors, the building's exterior is clad in the dark wooden planks typical for this region. The black color is achieved in an environmentally friendly manner, by heating the wood and without the use of synthetic varnish. The roof covering is traditional ceramic roof tiles, with a modern gray glaze and a simple shape.

"Thanks to the property's excellent orientation, the living spaces open up to the surrounding vistas."

HOUSE ON WINDY PEAK *by* STEMPEL & TESAR ARCHITECTS

LION'S PRIDE

CAPE TOWN, SOUTH AFRICA

Accessed from Kloof Road, which winds along the western slopes of Lion's Head, this site is positioned in the wind-protected suburb of Clifton and enjoys spectacular views over the sandy beaches, boulder outcrops, and Twelve Apostles mountains toward the south and sunset views over the Atlantic Ocean.

Not only did the architects have to address the steep slope, including excavation to accommodate the structure, but they needed to make the most of the incredible views. The home was conceived as an arrangement of staggered blocks that rise along the side of the mountain, with the upper, private levels becoming appropriately shielded from both visibility and street-level noise.

A vertically slatted box hovers over the terrace, allowing the forest bushwillow trees below to grow into this level, with screens that can be opened or closed to adjust the amount of natural dappled light filtering into the interior. The structure was engineered from a durable yet lightweight aluminum in a finish that mimics the different tones of bark, a sturdy solution to weathering Cape Town's capricious seasons.

The uppermost level, the master bedroom, sits above the treetops and as such the materials—white marble, pale timber—and use of skylights express a feeling of air and openness while foldaway glass walls welcome in the full expanse of the view. And with a view this amazing, it might be tricky to drag yourself away.

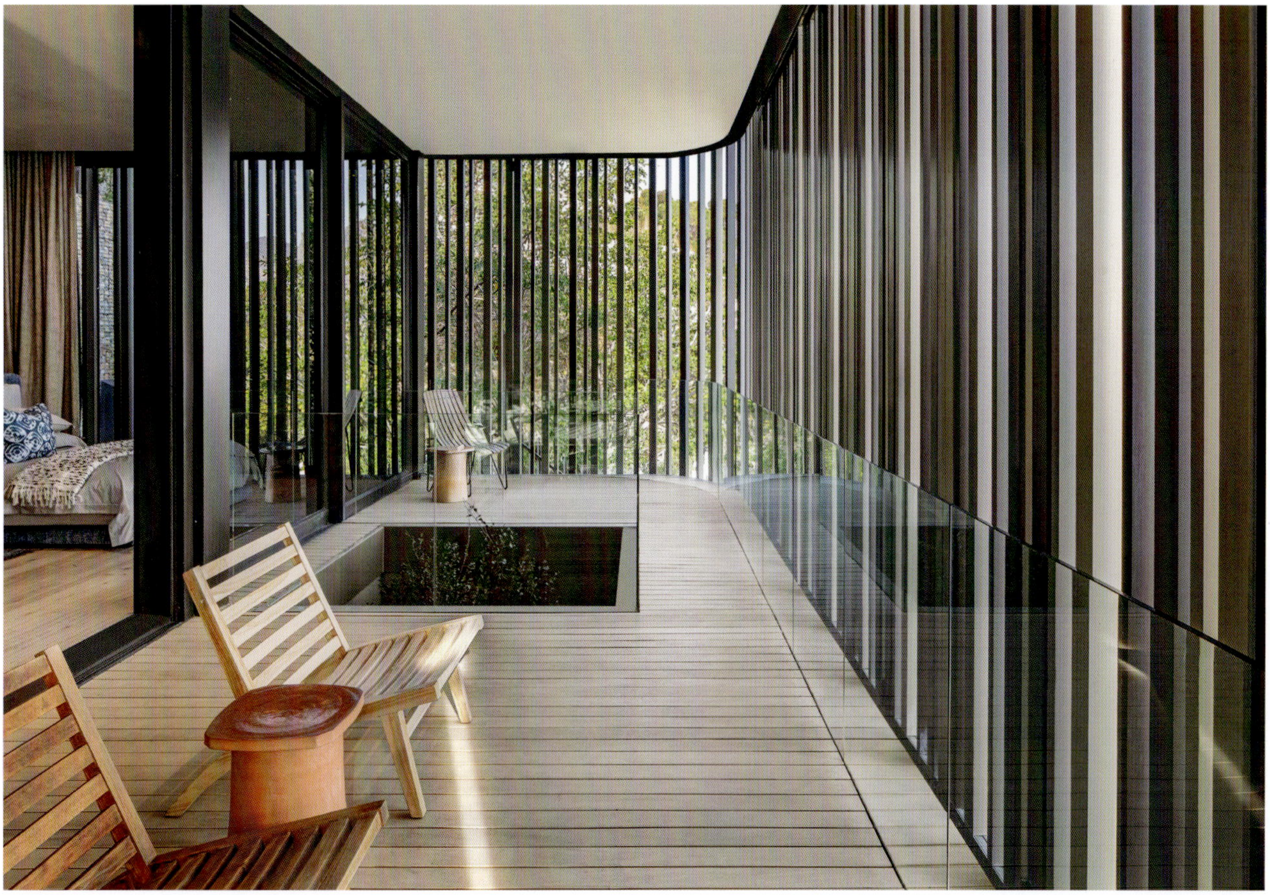

"A slatted box hovers over the terrace in a finish that mimics the different tones of bark."

KLOOF 145 *by* SAOTA

WINDSWEPT

JERSEY, UNITED KINGDOM

Not one but two modern houses enjoy this splendid setting on a stunning headland site on the island of Jersey, United Kingdom. Both houses are designed so as to blend into the surrounding landscape, allowing the surrounds to flow over parts of the house. And, with access to views this good, it was inevitable that these be prioritized by the designers.

Jersey is a small island off the north coast of France, and the houses rest in a beautiful headland setting, covered in native heather and gorse. The site itself is too windy and exposed to allow many trees to grow. In an effort to minimize the impact of the buildings, the structures are designed to "grow" out of the sloping site, with roof gardens placed on top.

The houses were both designed to be eco-friendly, with high levels of insulation, air-source heat pumps to provide low-energy heating, and photovoltaic cells with Tesla power walls for an off-grid existence.

A protected south-facing courtyard was created for the main house, which contains a natural swimming pool, one that is filtered by reeds and plants rather than a conventional chlorine system. The house is clad in a stone or slate that was also from the United Kingdom. The stone has an earthy feel and helps tie the buildings into the headland.

Not only can the inhabitants enjoy the beautiful colors of the English Channel (or, La Manche) stretching across the horizon, but they can do so in the comfort of the interior, warm and safe, away from the strong winds.

"Logie Point enjoys this splendid setting on a stunning headland site on the island of Jersey."

LOGIE POINT *by* GUZ ARCHITECTS

FLOATING ABOVE

LOS ANGELES, CA, UNITED STATES

Perched atop a Bel Air hilltop, this is an impressively modern and luxurious large custom residence steeped with intricacies designed to subtly "float" above its environs, and offer spectacular views of the city beneath.

Given its prominent positioning above a relatively developed neighborhood, the motivation behind the design of the home was to create a residence that could meld into its surroundings while maximizing views. The three-story structure is wrapped in glass that mirrors its sweeping views of the Los Angeles Basin, unobstructed, from the Getty Center to Long Beach, Century City, and Downtown. The huge panels provide a strong connection to nature and the seasonal arcs of light.

Balancing scale, views, and comfort proved to be the project's biggest challenge. The residence has been split into three levels, each consisting of three wings. The ground floor provides the entry and communal spaces for gathering, while the top floor is dedicated to the home's private spaces. The upper southwest and southeast wings are afforded 270-degree views of the city and ocean thanks to their slim profiles.

The glass curtain wall is a highly sophisticated system that required significant testing and innovation. It needed to not only offer protection against UV rays, but result in a beautiful varied glazed façade that would be reflective, opaque, and translucent as required.

But for all the technological know-how behind the engineering and careful placement of the layout, it is the sweeping views that justify the effort, both during the day and also at night, when the city lights below twinkle and wink.

"Perched atop a Bel Air hilltop, this impressively modern and luxurious residence offers spectacular views of the city."

ORUM RESIDENCE *by* SPF:ARCHITECTS

EASY LIVING

CAPE TOWN, SOUTH AFRICA

OVD525 is located on a steep mountainside site that boasts undisturbed views over Cape Town's Atlantic seaboard. The city is seen in the distance toward the east and the iconic Lion's Head Mountain towers over the house from the south. Western views take advantage of spectacular sunsets over the ocean.

The owner had already been living on the site, and bravely agreed to demolish the existing structure on the advice of the architects. In this way, the design could be tailored to the needs of the client, moreover unlocking the full potential of this privileged site, while creating complete privacy from nearby neighbors.

The house is conceived as a series of horizontal slabs containing gardens, decks, and pools that slide between two large-mass, shielding vertical elements at the flanking ends.

The master suite dramatically cantilevers over the external entertainment and pool area in order to capitalize on the views. It creates the planked concrete soffit of the main living level as it stretches out toward the horizon.

The architecture of this home has a restrained, natural material palette, and is respectful of the importance of the ever-changing city and ocean vistas. The house is conceived, detailed, and finished in an understated and unadorned manner, creating calm, flowing spaces that are easy to live in. The owner's decision to start again with a new design has been amply rewarded with beautiful views stretching over the Atlantic.

262

"OVD525 is located on a steep mountainside site that boasts undisturbed views over Cape Town's Atlantic seaboard."

OVD525 *by* THREE14ARCHITECTS

COASTAL ESCARPMENT

GERRINGONG, NSW, AUSTRALIA

Atelier Andy Carson excels in designing unusual residences that sit easily on verdant rolling hills, with broad outlooks. And The Range is no exception. This particular site has overwhelming views encompassing the ocean, the beach, a lagoon, a working farm, and a beautiful tall escarpment. Here, the landscape reigns surpreme, and provided an endless source of inspiration.

The clients originally longed for a modest two-bedroom residence with a basic farm shed–like appearance and the result was this beautiful yet simple home with a grounded connection to the farm and stunning sunset views of the Illawarra escarpment. The design here explores the vernacular steel frame building typology, referencing the typical farm shed buildings, as seen with the dairy sheds on the farm. The house becomes a reinterpretation of the modern farmhouse vernacular. The western façade contains a standout feature, namely the large operable copper panels, which can be adjusted to allow full control of light and the views of the beautiful sunsets.

With a simple floor-plan and a primary axis aligned north-south to make the best use of the ocean views to the southern side, and the green rolling hills of a pastoral paradise to the north, the residence offers a comfortable and tranquil sanctuary, evoking a sense of calm.

From the entrance to the building, a framed view through the home to the ocean is created, giving a hint at what is yet to come. From the central dining area, views to the beach, lagoon, and coast sweep over the wooden decking. Moving through the minimally decorated building, there are constant little surprises but also interesting angles and new views to be had from the secure comfort of the interior.

"The landscape reigns surpreme, and provided an endless source of inspiration."

THE RANGE *by* ATELIER ANDY CARSON

MOUNTAINSIDE MARVEL

MASSIF DU CHARLEVOIX, QC, CANADA

Set in a wintery landscape, this holiday home will eventually become the main residence of the owners for their retirement years, but until then it is the location for family gatherings and vacation fun, including skiing.

The approach is via a sinuous and winding road, which offers the final reward of a sweeping view down over the sloping treed hillsides to the Saint Lawrence River and beyond.

The front façade of the entrance is discreet and non-assuming, allowing the transparent façade of the other side to take precedence. Here, the long view across the countryside fittingly bestows upon the home its name.

The rooms are set in an enfilade, which culminates in the grand gallery with its spectacular vistas. In warmer months the residents can enjoy their incredible lookout from the veranda that encircles the rear of the house. Bedecked with pale-white pine floorboards and ceiling, contrasted with modern black window frames and lighting fixtures, the interior design reinforces the impression of projecting and focusing attention toward the horizon.

This residence, judiciously placed on a plateau on the side of the mountain, proposes a simple but effective appreciation of the countryside through its location parallel to the river. The linear form of the house and the organization of the interior rooms along with exterior additions allow the inhabitants to benefit from the different qualities of the site year-round and at any moment of the day. And naturally the tranquility of the outstanding views.

"The long view across the countryside fittingly bestows upon the home its name."

RÉSIDENCE LA LONGUE VUE *by* BOURGEOIS / LECHASSEUR ARCHITECTES

NATURAL INTEGRATION

JACKSON HOLE, WY, UNITED STATES

Nestled into the top of Gros Ventre Ridge, this home is intended to embrace nature, and integrate the architecture within its natural context. The site itself was carefully selected for its breathtaking panoramic views.

Each room overlooks the Grand Teton mountain range and the adjacent valleys, offering sweeping views to the far horizon. The view outside changes throughout the seasons but is always consistently stunning and captivating.

The main roofline follows the natural slope of the land, and provides protection from the harsh western sun and the driving snows. The central exterior terrace is located under the roof, providing shelter from strong winds, and snow that can accumulate in massive drifts. The entire structure is deliberately kept relatively close to the ground. The garage is built into the hillside and is covered with a green roof to allow the natural sage, grasses, and wildflowers to return to the site.

The interior is contemporary and modern, yet simple in design so as not to draw attention away from the glorious expanses visible through the floor-to-ceiling glass windows. From either within the warm and cozy interior, or settled comfortably in a lounging chair in the protected terrace, the view set out before you of the looming mountains and the valley floor is striking. What a place to watch the clouds roll over the peaks.

"The site itself was carefully selected for its breathtaking panoramic views."

RIDGELINE RESIDENCE *by* WELCH HALL ARCHITECTS

VINEYARD BEAUTY

HEALDSBURG, CA, UNITED STATES

Sitting on top of a hill overlooking Healdsburg, this modest house reposes gently in the landscape. This home offers both ample social space ideal for entertaining and the privacy of a rural retreat, but one blessed with sweeping views. It's the perfect place to relax and unwind, lulled into a sense of tranquility by the vision of mature trees and distant hills as the wind rustles through the tall grass.

The taller section runs along the ridge of the hill and houses the home's great room under lofty ceilings, expansive floor-to-ceiling glazing, and a simple shed overhanging roof, filled with light and views let in through tall glass walls. Four oversized glass panels open dramatically on each side, transforming the space into an outdoor pavilion whose flush concrete floors extend into a poolside patio to the north and a terrace and a fire pit to the south, offering comfortable outdoor areas for both hot and cool weather. With these doors drawn up, the outdoors truly becomes part of the interior, while the site offers one continuous view from the pool, through the great room, and down into the distant village below.

With dark-stained cedar siding and low stone landscape walls that anchor the building, Sonoma Wine Country 1 offers a modest and thoughtful response to both its site and the client's needs. Just imagine enjoying the views with a chilled glass of Chardonnay from one of the surrounding Sonoma vineyards, preferably at dusk to fully benefit from the awe-inspiring sunsets.

"With these doors drawn up, the outdoors truly becomes part of the interior, while the site offers one long continuous view."

SONOMA WINE COUNTRY I *by* FELDMAN ARCHITECTURE

ARRANGING THE VIEW

VANCOUVER, BC, CANADA

The first request of the new owners of this mountainside lot was that no land was to be cleared before the design had been formed. The architect took the opportunity to camp on-site to absorb the nuances of the land and setting, and discover the potential views.

The house is designed to be one with the land. Natural materials such as local stone and timber are used. A post-and-beam structural system maximizes the capture of the views. Clean simple lines and the fine balance of wood versus raw concrete materials satisfy the warm modern aesthetic preferred by the owners.

Views are revealed slowly, with axial views along hallways to significant landmarks, including Mount Baker in the Cascade Ranges. A walk around the house offers a visual journey through the beautiful immediate, mid-range, and distant horizon.

Once comfortably ensconced in the house, the owners and their guests exhibit little desire to leave. And who can blame them.

"The house is designed to be one with the land."

SPINY GROUSE *by* FWC ARCHITECTURE

SEASIDE SERENITY

NHA TRANG, VIETNAM

Located in Nha Trang, a seaside city on Vietnam's southeast coastline, this vacation villa enjoys a privileged location. Carved into the hill, it captures unique views overlooking the bay and mountains beyond.

The overall design emphasizes simplistic forms, the use of raw and natural materials, and innovative interior functions. The exterior has a prominent brutalist influence while, contrastingly, the interiors are timber-laden, warm, and grounding.

A coarsely carved sculptural stone wall at the back of the property makes reference to the surrounding rocky environment. The front façade is completely opaque and orients radically toward the sea. An array of shadows and light dance across the granite blocks, adding drama and effect while also establishing a bold and exciting identity from the street.

From the infinity pool to the master bedroom (with a retractable glass loggia to provide a fully immersive sea and stars viewing), the design strives to connect the sky and the scenery with the sense of space of the building. The primary goal of the villa's design is to maximize the beauty of the scenery, which can be enjoyed from just about every corner of the home.

"The beauty of the scenery can be enjoyed from just about every corner of the home."

STONE HOUSE *by* MM++ARCHITECTS

CONNECTING THE VIEWS

VANCOUVER, BC, CANADA

Located on a steep and technically challenging site, this project is designed to capture immediate views of heavy marine traffic and the open sea to the west.

Movement through the house is choreographed to disguise considerable elevation change from the street to the main living spaces. The split-level arrangement coupled with the consolidation of the upper floor to one side of the building allowed for generously tall main living spaces and a close connection between the upper and main floors.

The client wanted a house that had an expression of draft and materiality. Heavily revealed board-formed concrete shows a soft wood-grain texture and mimics the natural wood used throughout. Concrete at the roof level creates the feeling that the space is solid and sculptured rather than assembled from a series of pieces.

The opening created by this massive concrete frame generates a rudimentary connection to the sea and sky. Spaces feel simultaneously open and contained. It's the perfect location for watching the ships as they perform their water-bourne ballet, moving in and out.

"This project is designed to capture immediate views of marine traffic and the open sea."

SUNSET HOUSE *by* MCCLEOD BOVELL MODERN HOUSES

LOFTY GLAMOR

LOS ANGELES, CA, UNITED STATES

Trousdale Residence is the result of the search for a site with dramatic views and sunny exposures on which to build a beautiful home. Set high in the hills above Beverly Hills, this new home makes the most of open spaces and, of course, that view.

The main body of the house intentionally opens to the southwest, so that every room has a panoramic vista, all the way to the ocean. With large, retractable glass doors, this side also opens physically to the outdoors, expanding the living area of the house. A large great room occupies the center of the plan with a prime view of the city. At 40 feet (12 meters) long, it includes seating and dining areas and a bar, all inviting the room to be used day into night. There is a parallel open space for the kitchen and breakfast area, also looking onto the view and the pool. On the other side of the great room, a sequestered master suite is set down a few steps, with a glass corner that opens directly to the pool.

Typical of designs produced by Studio William Hefner, Trousdale oozes luxurious comfort and quality, resulting in a modern yet laid-back home where every room is given access to the wonderful views that result from its glorious location.

"This new home is on a site with dramatic views and sunny exposures."

TROUSDALE RESIDENCE *by* STUDIO WILLIAM HEFNER

PERENNIAL BLISS

ISTEBNA, POLAND

Responding to a request from the clients to design a unique destination for family gatherings, Blueroom produced this contemporary villa that merges traditional vernacular design with the progressive ideas of the client, along with a focus on providing maximum access to the views beyond.

The villa makes the most of its stunning rural location, with spacious views across the green countryside to the Beskidy Mountains in the country's south. Generous windows frame the panoramic view to the green valley and dramatize the layered experience of the mountain range. All the bedrooms have contextual color schemes, based on the rich color palette of local mosses.

The interior design is decidedly contemporary, with sharp lines and a muted color palette, so as not to distract from the exterior views. The glass façade can be opened, uniting the living room with the perimeter veranda in one uninterrupted luxurious terrace.

The wood was all sourced locally, and the garden will be restored to its natural former state with a rich mix of local vegetation. The traditional shingled roof, reflecting the archetypal houses found all through the region, cantilevers out to offer protection from the weather.

Through the merging of contemporary sharp lines, a vernacular sheltering roof shape, and a maximum focus on view and openness, this villa offers a constantly changing sensory experience of its surroundings, in any weather and in all seasons.

"Generous windows frame the panoramic view to the green valley and dramatize the layered experience of the mountain range."

VERANDA VILLA *by* BLUEROOM

SERIES OF VIEWS

PAROS, GREECE

Located on the beautiful Cycladic island of Paros, this house faces west, toward the sea and the views.

The structure protrudes from the natural slope, and is aligned on a cantilever slab that floats over the land. On the eastern side lays the patio, protected from the northern winds, providing the perfect spot to soak up the sun and drink in the view. The entrance to the house is placed on the westernmost point of the plot. The back yard nestles in the core space between the buildings and the slope, and it extends toward the south side to meet the patio. It is the intermediate between the natural and the built, and between the main house, the common areas, the guest house, and the patio.

The buildings reinterpret the basic elements of the Cycladic architecture: white volumes interconnect with open spaces, but this time they rest on a cantilever platform, an observation point that touches the earth lightly, with a view toward the neighboring island of Antiparos and the hillside that plunges into the Aegean. The platform was part of a pre-existing agricultural terrace, integrated with the natural landscape and altered to create a contemporary architectural point of interest.

The house is designed as a series of frames toward the view, thus turning the building into a "viewing machine." And while this relaxed dwelling may indeed be a "viewing machine," it is also an object that itself both welcomes and is subject to observation.

"The house is designed as a series of frames toward the view."

VIEWMASTER *by* REACT ARCHITECTS

EAGLE'S VIEWPOINT

MALLORCA, SPAIN

Sited on a hilltop, with views to die for, this house is described poetically by the architects as being an eagle's nest in the mountain, with a connection to the sky.

With its dramatic topography and fabulous views, the designers were keen to take full advantage of the plot and location. And so was the client, who requested that the 360-degree panoramic views were fully maximized, but also that the resulting home was private. The design strategy projects the house out of the hill as much as possible; the house "flies out" of the mountain with a dramatic cantilever, providing a sense of privacy from the street but also opening up to all the views of the valley, mountains, and the sea beyond.

Access to the home is through a plaza at the back. In this way, the views are hidden, so to surprise visitors once they are inside the house. Indeed, all the vistas open up once inside the house, providing a full panoramic view of the valley and the sea. The pool with its infinity edge seemingly brings the distant sea closer to the house.

By projecting the first floor out as much as possible a shelter-shade opportunity is given to the ground floor, so the living areas are protected from the strong Mediterranean sun.

All the bedrooms have an outdoor terrace, while the roof has been rendered as a deck (for what else could it be at this incredible hilltop location?), and provides extra sitting and lounge areas, all with breathtaking views.

"The pool with its infinity edge seemingly brings the distant sea closer to the house."

WHERE EAGLES DARE *by* GRAS REYNÉS ARCHITECTURE STUDIO

PROJECT CREDITS

SWEEPING BAY VIEWS 12–19
A House with a View
Axelrod Architects
axelrodarchitects.com
Photography: Bruce Damonte Photography

RELAXED VISTAS 20–27
Above the Lake
Dick Clark + Associates
dcarch.com
Photography Dror Baldinger, FAIA

REVISITING TRADITION 28–35
AP House Urbino
GGA gardini gibertini architetti
gardini-gibertini.it
Photography Ezio Manciucca

ATLANTIC VISION 36–43
Beyond
SAOTA
saota.com
Photography Adam Letch

RIVER CANYON 44–51
Blue Jay Way
McClean Design
mccleandesign.com
Photography Berlyn Photography

PANORAMIC PERFECTION 52–59
Casa Ambar
Centerbrook
centerbrook.com
Photography Peter Aaron/OTTO

ALIEN LANDSCAPE 60–67
Casa C3
Barclay & Crousse Architecture
barclaycrousse.com
Photography Cristóbal Palma

SOARING ABOVE 68–75
Devlin
McClean Design
mccleandesign.com
Photography Jim Bartsch, Berlyn Photography

ORGANIC SCULPTURE 76–83
Elliptic House
Mário Martins Atelier
mariomartins.com
Photography Fernando Guerra FG+SG Architectural Photography

FRAMING THE VIEW 84–91
Frame House
Nomo Studio
nomostudio.eu
Photography Adrià Goula

ON EVERY LEVEL 92–99
Greenacres
Austin Maynard Architects
maynardarchitects.com
Photography Tess Kelly

BRIDGE BETWEEN 100–7
H_Orizon
Vois Architects
voisarchitects.com
Photography Erietta Attali, Athina Souli

ON SOLID ROCK 108–17
House on Formentera Island
Marià Castelló Martínez
m-ar.net
Photography Marià Castelló Martínez

THE INFINITE SEA 116–23
House of the Infinite
Alberto Campo Baeza
campobaeza.com
Photography Javier Callejas

CARIBBEAN IDYLL 124–31
House on a Dune
Oppenheim Architecture
oppenoffice.com
Photography Karen Fuchs, Patricia Parinejad

SIMPLE DECEPTION 132–39
House on Windy Peak
Stempel & Tesar Architects
stempel-tesar.com
Photography Filip Šlapal

LION'S PRIDE 140–47
Kloof 145
SAOTA
saota.com
Photography Adam Letch

WINDSWEPT 148–55
Logie Point
Guz Architects
guzarchitects.com
Photography Patrick Bingham-Hall

FLOATING ABOVE 156–65
Orum Residence
SPF:Architects
spfa.com
Photography Matthew Momberger

EASY LIVING 166–73
OVD525
Three14Architects
three14.co.za
Photography Adam Letch

COASTAL ESCARPMENT 174–81
The Range
Atelier Andy Carson
atelier-andy-carson.com
Photography Tom Blachford & Kate Ballis, Michael Nicholson

MOUNTAINSIDE MARVEL 182–89
Résidence la Longue Vue
Bourgeois / Lechasseur architectes
bourgeoislechasseur.com
Photography Adrien Williams

NATURAL INTEGRATION 190–97
Ridgeline Residence
Welch Hall Architects
welchhall.com
Photography Dror Baldinger, FAIA

VINEYARD BEAUTY 198–205
Sonoma Wine Country 1
Feldman Architecture
feldmanarchitecture.com
Photography Joe Fletcher

ARRANGING THE VIEW 206–13
Spiny Grouse
FWC Architecture
fwcarchitecture.com
Photography Peter Powles

SEASIDE SERENITY 214–21
Stone House
MM++ Architects
mmarchitects.net
Photography Hiroyuki Oki

CONNECTING THE VIEWS 222–29
Sunset House
McLeod Bovell Modern Houses
mcleodbovell.com
Photography Ema Peter, Martin Tessler

LOFTY GLAMOR 230–37
Trousdale Residence
Studio William Hefner
williamhefner.com
Photography James Ray Spahn

PERENNIAL BLISS 238–45
Veranda Villa
Blueroom
blueroom.design
Photography Igor Kozłowski

SERIES OF VIEWS 246–53
Viewmaster
React Architects
re-act.gr
Photography George Messaritakis

EAGLE'S VIEWPOINT 254–61
Where Eagles Dare
GRAS Reynés Architecture Studio
grasarquitectos.com
Photography José Hevia Photography

First reprinted 2022
The Images Publishing Group Reference Number: 1635

First published in Australia in 2021 by
The Images Publishing Group Pty Ltd
ABN 89 059 734 431

Offices

Melbourne
6 Bastow Place
Mulgrave, Victoria 3170
Australia
Tel: +61 3 9561 5544

New York
6 West 18th Street 4B
New York, NY 10011
United States
Tel: +1 212 645 1111

Shanghai
6F, Building C, 838 Guangji Road
Hongkou District, Shanghai 200434
China
Tel: +86 021 31260822

books@imagespublishing.com
www.imagespublishing.com

All photography is attributed in the Project Credits on pages 262–63, unless otherwise noted. Pages 2–3: Fernando Guerra FG+SG Architectural Photography (Mário Martins Atelier, Elliptic House); page 4: Adam Letch (SAOTA, Kloof 145); page 6: Joe Fletcher (Feldman Architecture, Sonoma Wine Country 1); page 8: Ezio Manciucca (GGA gardini gibertini architetti, AP House Urbino)

NATIONAL LIBRARY OF AUSTRALIA

A catalogue record for this book is available from the National Library of Australia

Title: Infinity House: An endless view
Author: Cathi House [Introduction]
ISBN: 9781864708622

FSC www.fsc.org MIX Paper from responsible sources FSC® C019910

Printed and bound in China by Artron Art Group on 157gsm Chinese OJI matte art paper
Prepress by A&S Press, Singapore